# From Glory to Glory…

## The poetry of
## Theresa Marie Cain

## Volume 1
## Reflections from My Experiences

Copyright

From Glory to Glory
By Theresa Marie Cain

All rights reserved. No part of this publication may be reproduced or transmitted in any form or by any means without written permission of the writer.

**Dedication**

I dedicate this book to my Family...
Even in all of our struggles, God is still changing us from glory to glory

My daughter Iyana, my gift from God.
Veronica Cain, the most accepting mother a woman could have.
Deborah McCampbell, for her loving support and Christ-like encouragement.

And to all those friends and family who have <u>consistently</u> been there for me no matter how hard. Thanks for walking in His love with me always!

From Glory to Glory...

"But we all, with unveiled face, beholding as in a mirror the glory of the Lord, are being transformed into the same image from glory to glory, just as by the Spirit of the Lord."

**2 Corinthians 3:18**

**Table of Contents**

Foreword ..................................................................9

Introduction ...........................................................11

**Glory One:** Man's Rejection vs. Christ's Acceptance

    Faithfulness: God vs. Man ...........................14

    My Lesson Learned .......................................16

    Walk in Love....................................................18

    Not Available .................................................20

    The Cost of the Critical Spirit ......................22

    Invisible............................................................24

    Purity of Heart ...............................................26

    What? ..............................................................29

    My Sufficiency is Not in You .......................35

**Glory Two:** Singleness vs. Contentment

    Covenant Love ...............................................40

    Fairy Tales .......................................................42

    Now Whole .....................................................44

    This Ain't No Dating Thing ...........................47

    What's taking God so long? .........................48

    Contentment .................................................50

    Christ Saves.....................................................51

My Promise Land ...... 53

Done ...... 56

Resignation ...... 57

Memories ...... 58

Not Giving Up ...... 60

Boundaries ...... 62

Something New ...... 64

**Glory Three:** Lust of the Flesh vs. Surrendering to the Spirit

My Hope ...... 68

Depth ...... 69

Surrender, Not Excusing Sin ...... 71

I Ain't Lookin Back ...... 75

Am I Sure ...... 77

Is That All You Want? ...... 79

**Glory Four:** Bondage of Religion vs. Liberty of Relationship.

Worship, Not Religion ...... 88

Distortion ...... 90

Freedom in Christ ...... 92

You've Been a Friend ...... 94

Sometimes I Wonder ...... 96

**Glory Five:** Worry & Uncertainty vs. Patience & Purpose

    The Deposit ................................................100

    I AM ..........................................................101

    Expectation ...............................................103

    Wait on the Lord! .......................................105

    Reign .........................................................106

    Transition ..................................................107

    Conceding My Will .....................................109

    Why Worry? ...............................................111

    Whose Confused? ......................................113

**Glory Six:** Character of Christ

    Enthroned .................................................116

    Relentless ..................................................119

    His Face .....................................................122

    Rhema .......................................................123

    Great God ..................................................124

    Chains .......................................................126

    He is Christ ................................................129

    My Letter to God .......................................131

    Scriptures to Build Faith .............................132

    Author Info ................................................136

## Foreword

This collection of Spirit-led spoken word & poetry will introduce you to Theresa M. Cain, affectionately known to me as "Ms. T". She is an extraordinary single mom who faces daily the challenges and struggles of choosing to live a Christian lifestyle. Her words come from a personal journey of spiritual highs and lows leading to triumphant deliverance!

These poems are soulful, spiritual works that will captivate your heart and speak to your inner spirit. She will emotionally draw you into God's presence with her honesty about life's reality and the healing truth shared will compel you to search the very depths of your soul. Seeing God work miracles in her life, and watching her spiritual growth has been a joy to behold. What I love most about Theresa is her ability to hear truth and even when she doesn't feel like it she will surrender to it because she loves the Lord with all her heart. Her poems are evidence that God is living, moving and breathing in her life and she desires to share her joy with the world.

When you begin to read, and savor a taste of her poetry, your thirsty soul will yearn for more!

"Oh Taste and See That the Lord Is Good!" Psalms 34:8
May His Spirit Continue to Reign in Your Hearts Until He Comes Again!
In His Spirit, Deborah McCampbell

## Introduction

This body of work is an expression of who I am. It includes the pain I have experienced through rejection, singleness, temptations, and worry. There is an attempt in my writing to also share Christ's acceptance of me, contentment, surrender, liberty, patience, purpose and the character of Christ. My approach is to express a balance between all of the things I struggle with and God's faithfulness in them.

I pray that these poems will touch you...
I pray they will encourage, edify and exhort.
I pray they will convict, liberate and release.
I hope some will even make you laugh.
I pray that these words and the healing Spirit that are shared in will be a balm and a blessing...

In all we go through, good, bad, and ugly, we are being shaped into His image from glory to glory.

In His love, Theresa Marie Cain

"But the Lord said to Samuel, "Do not look on his appearance or on the height of his stature, because I have rejected him. For the Lord sees not as man sees: man looks on the outward appearance, but the Lord looks on the heart."

1 Samuel 16:7

**Glory 1**

**Man's Rejection**

**vs.**

**Christ's Acceptance**

## Faithfulness: God vs. Man

Walking when others try to knock you down

Intimidated by your smile

They make you frown

Your light makes them aware of the darkness they walk

Revealing their sin, at you they balk

Interacting in love is what you try to do

Blinded by envy can't see your heart true

The pain of rejection already in place

Made worse by "friends" actions make you hide your face

Avoiding interaction

Fearing the worst

The sincerity of actions which seem so rehearsed

Wanting healing so Christ's light can still shine

Soul dimmed by pain & wrong thoughts in the mind

Keeping you cloistered

Secluded and lacking in trust

Because the fruit of their lips is a lie

Turns to dust

Wanting to believe someone cares if you're down
Not many reach out so the doubts still abound

The Holy Spirit is quietly taking His turn
To use each negative situation as a lesson to learn
His aim in all things is to foster character, growth
To build patience, love, and Christ-like methods to cope

He knows what you feel is real and yes, He cares
Take His yoke which is easy
Your burdens He bares
These lessons are invaluable
Meditate every day
When fears & pain arise His sweet joy pushes away

Don't daily battle the unfaithfulness of man
Don't block Christ's love
Just walk in His plans

**My Lesson Learned**

Love Unconditional-Agape
Feeling in a microscopic, miniscule way
What it means to love and not receive it
Believing in something and grieve to lose it
Jesus! Our incarnate God! Emmanuel!
Came to save us all and by sin He fell
Not welcome because their perceptions were flawed
And finally...I understand His pain-I am awed
Can only imagine the weight
The tears of blood that rained at the rejection He'd face
To His holiness it would a be a terrible affront
The pain and agony He would confront-What He carried?
The brunt of all our sin before and sin to come
I have tasted a small part of it
Christ the Son in bearing it fully was the only One
To know the agony of denial and faces turned away
Afraid to say they know His name
Darkness took over the brightness of day
His stature bowed low
His shoulders bow under the weight of chastisement
I feel the sting, my Lord, of the punishment you received

An advertisement of just how forgiven are we
I can conceive what you faced having someone walk away
Abandoned and bound, confined in a way that I am no longer free-I can see
Nailed into His hands and poured out of His pierced sides
Shedding all deity where in Him it always resides
The Father's love showered & people wouldn't believe
Couldn't receive His sacrifice for their sin blinded eyes
He grieves
Lord forgive them for they know not what they do
Giving His all to only get a crown of thorns
Sour wine to appease His thirst
What blood burst from your veins that you would set down your reign
Still He satisfied the worst sin with the payment of Himself
Bore such pain for us…
He allowed me to feel in a microscopic, miniscule way
So that I can learn just what a sacrifice He made
Learning to love unconditionally
What an amazing grace

**Walk in Love...**

Life is too short to not walk in love
Remembering the eternal sacrifice from God above
Spotless lamb, slaughtered for my sin
Now I carry His Spirit within
Longing to share His care & concern with friends
Learning from broken fellowship, seeking to restore
Longing for connection, knocking on Friendship's door
Wondering when to shake the dust from my feet & walk away
How can we connect? What can I say?
Talk is cheap and faith without works dead
Yet His sheep so full of words and regret over what should have been said
No relational fruit & only selfish ambition
False affection and insincere interaction
Rehearsed renditions of "God bless you" & "I'll be praying for you"
The smile fades as their heads turn eschew
Not burning with a desire to bear one another's burdens
And overwhelming urge to retreat prevails
Claiming to hail Jesus as Lord, from their presence I bail

Yet failing time and time again to show His love, grand delusions of peace
False illusions I wish would cease
I want a release from relational mediocrity, dissonance
To be welcomed into the warm embrace of loving covenant
Ah...
But only through Christ's holy sacrament & complete surrender to Him
Can we abandon selfish ambitions and desires within?
Love a neighbor and die for a friend
Make a sacrifice that though it won't save from sin
Can change the life of a man or woman
Life is too short to not walk in love...

**Not Available**

I am a woman with choices
Not moving at the holler and hail of voices
I can be available when I want to be
Don't have to be around for your every beck and call
I need peace to be free
Have a moment to pick myself up when I fall
Can't depend on you to be my source
That position is already taken by a loving God
He demands my all
Whose kingdom cannot be shaken!
Whose love has never forsaken!
Even in times of loneliness
In the desperation of pain
Only He remains
Yet…I want to dial the phone
I know my mom is there
I await your call
I want to know you care
This pain alone I cannot bare
Yet I find myself calling the Lord's name
I'm reminded to keep my faith in Christ

In Him I must remain

In no friend can I put complete trust

Even friends and family can disappoint with their fallible,

selfish, fickle natures

We, yes me, focus on our own wants and lusts

As I grow older, I'm learning to enjoy the quiet

Learning to not be dependent

Fasting from this diet of other's opinions and ideas

Solitude

Peace

Contentment in Christ means that others do not provide

my soul's release

I want to learn to stand on my own two feet

I want to be complete and let God meet my needs

Don't be offended at all

If I take some time with Jesus...

And don't answer when you call

## The Cost of the Critical Spirit

Do you know what it feels like to experience the sting or
burn of critical & condemning eyes?
Who judge on the outward, ignoring the inward & attack
with hate & despise
Not seeking the heart & can't recognize the spirit within
who seeks to honor Christ
Instead coming with words that tear down & destroy
without regard to the unholy price
Walking in love is not their agenda but seeking to find
what is wrong
Prying for info to bring judgment & censure, discouraging
others as they move along
Your hair is too long, your skirt is too short, how dare you
wear red on 1st Sunday?
You worship too loud, don't you dance with such passion,
is that tongues with which I hear you pray?
Your hands always raised, you're blocking my view, can
you sit down so I can see?
Am I blocking your view of all you wish to subdue with
your mouth full of vicious decree?
The pastor preaches on love and walking in forgiveness

and corrects those that don't practice the truth.
You loudly say amen, turn to a buddy and say it again not realizing that he's talking to you!
Left in your wake are the hearts you have broken and the spirits you've crushed with your hate.
Not thinking that maybe your words have done damage and that your opinion should not dominate.
I leave with you these words from our Holy Scriptures, the book that should guide our whole lives.
Jesus says love one another so that we can represent Him and this command you should not despise.
For how can the world come to know of His love when we can't even show it amongst ourselves?
Let us work with all diligence to follow this path and leave the doctrine of criticism on the shelf!

## Invisible

God, you love me so why am I invisible?
You have never left nor forsaken me yet the longing to be
seen, accepted, validated and valued has shaken me.
On the fringe, I just want to belong
I feel I've been treated so wrong
How can I know so clearly the depth & width of your care
for me yet not be able to grasp hold of my worth?
I have no mirth
Sometimes feeling like a stranger on this big earth
Does anyone see me?
On the periphery, I am ignored and outcast when God has
gifted me so abundantly to reveal His glory
I want to tell my story to a friend but am cloistered
secluded, and withdrawn
The appreciation from His people doesn't last long
It's nice to occasionally be recognized
Can I get a Hi?
A few more people with which I can verbalize?
Dreading checking the phone for fear of no messages
missed

Always at home because who is there to spend time with?
Hearing the dial tone and hanging up because there is no one to call
Sometimes the tears fall at how lonely I am
No boyfriend and besides my daughter no companion
An enemy inspired response is hide my light and face
When around others expediently & hurried I leave because my light in full bloom I'm worried won't be seen
I am afraid of the rejection I might receive
I am deceived into thinking that if I just leave...
The fear lingers still...
Why can't you love the fullness of me?
Diminished, withdrawn, you are led to show concern completely
I want to bask in God's glory and operate in His plan fully
In my insecurity I see you run from me
Behind closed doors criticize me
At least that's what I think
On the brink of hiding away forever
Lord, I just want to be seen...the way you see me!

## Purity of Heart

"To the pure all things are pure, but to those who are corrupted and do not believe, nothing is pure..." Titus 1:15

I want my heart to be pure in all I say and do
But many times the eyes of man cannot accept this truth
They're blinded by the surface flesh
Do not see beyond
My spirit seeks to honor God yet they ignore our bond
Why do they judge me on personality or what I choose to wear?
What difference does it make if I wear tall heels or braided hair?
1 Samuel 16:7 speaks exactly to this point
He has called me as His chosen one
I'm who He did anoint
My Lord does not see me by appearances
Outward displays
He looks into my heart and soul
My walk with Him He weighs
I love the Lord with my being
Wish that they could see

That as His workmanship and prize I have liberty
Galatians 1 & 10 does say, "For if I still pleased men...I would not be Christ's servant."
And this truth I don't pretend
The approval of man I do not wish to have nor do I seek
To carry myself with boldness as in Christ I'm made complete
No man has shed his blood for me
No woman's back was scarred
Nor did their hands shape in the womb the baby who I was
Not in man's image was I formed
No breath in me did man breathe
Both egg and seed that God created was how I was conceived
So when a man or woman seeks to dictate who I am
On Christ my rock and solid Word
Sure foundation do I stand
I revel in my freedom here
In worship some may lack
I try to ignore others who talk behind my back

Praise is not an area where any should have slack
Paul says don't be a stumbling block
Not to Christians, Gentile or Jew
But I won't be put in bondage to please you or you or you
This is a practice we must all embrace to honor Christ
It's not about personality but a reflection of your life
At some point balance must be found as God has strengthened me
To no more carry my head low if folks don't approve of T

## What?

You don't want me?
A woman filled with the righteousness of God in Christ
How can that be?
Beautiful masterpiece
Created in Christ Jesus for good works
Why can't you see?
Where has perception been so distorted that she who walks holy is no longer the prize?
You look at me with shock and disdain in your eyes when I rebuff your attempts to rub up my thighs
You think I'm easily going to fall for your flattery and lies
My God has already warned me to look out for the enemy who is always in disguise
Tall, dark and handsome you may be
Might be light skinned but through you I see
That smile, blinding is drawing me but the Holy Spirit at my shirt tail is tugging me
Roaming about like a roaring lion
Who are you seeking to devour, destroy?
Not valuing a woman for the good things she is
Treating her like a dollar store toy

You're just letting me know how much of a boy you are

Petulant and whining

With your pressuring and cajoling

It's akin to crying as your character is defining

Having a temper tantrum because you can't have a piece

of my candy

Walking with Christ sure comes in handy

Like Avatar I can see you

As I know who I am in Him more and more

I can pick up the pieces of me you were trying to hijack

and walk out the door

My heart is less broken at your rejection

No more content with your inappropriate affections

Attempting to treat me like I'm a whore

I WON'T LET YOU

You need to find something else to do

I am the apple of my Daddy's eye

Don't you dare try to reduce me to the size of my breasts,

hips and thighs!

I can almost even sympathize with your struggle knowing

women nowadays

They get your mind to wondering

Setting your thoughts ablaze

Seducing

Tantalizing

Enticing with their eyes

Manipulating with their sexuality

Employing tactics with their alluring cries

Like the woman in Proverbs looking to entrap a man with her disguise

Forget that for a minute

Focus on what needs to be realized

Not the temporary pleasure and sexual highs

Would you like to know me instead of trying to coerce me to compromise?

Listen very carefully to the words that I must say

Hey, turn your eyes to mine

Stop looking for a conquest to lay

Nothing about me communicates quick and easy here

Steer clear of this potted clay that Jesus Christ loves so dear

Died so that in safety I might to His hem adhere

Molded with a destiny far greater than your temporary attempts to play
I have people who love me praying for me every day
You might be the carrier of a weapon being formed against me yet you won't prosper
Swallowed up by the Spirit of God like a big man eats a whopper
I am His anointed one
A girl you will not touch
I promise it'll come back to bite and it will hurt very much
What's working through you cannot win
Please treat me like a lady
Like I have the spirit of God within
Can't you see that he's speaking through me?
Offering you the truth
The boundaries I set aren't to communicate that I'm a puritan or a prude
There are spiritual systems in place abounding with protection
Our lives should be the proof of a Christ centered connection

Principals taught to me in my youth and probably you too
And like the prodigal daughter for a moment I strayed like you
Tempted and distracted by my own insecure ways
I am back with a vengeance
My dignity here to stay
How about you think of joining me in this race?
Can you dedicate yourself to doing something distinct?
Maybe talk a Bible course or do something disparate?
There is a greater gift in God that we can inherit
Can your heart be softened to receive the seed I'm trying to plant?
Can you see yourself not being controlled by the member in your pants?
Can you look beyond your arousal to the potential to build something more than just a climax?
And then it crosses my mind
I am so thankful that Christ loves and accepts me
As hard as it may be to understand at times
He has given me everything I need
If the foundation of who I am was built on every "you"

I'd be a pile of crushed sea shells on the sand without value
Being walked on and lied upon
That's a life I must eschew
Stepped on and over by every man looking for a distraction
I am made for much more than just a temporary attraction
I'm built for lasting relationship and permanent interaction
You don't want me
That's ok
You don't get the satisfaction

## My Sufficiency Is Not In You

If God's grace is sufficient for me why can't it be sufficient for you
You are not required to judge and condemn me for every little thing I do
If sin is not the source of your desire to converse
Then your words and criticisms, unnecessary debates will only make things worse
Anything that's not in love or truth you wish to say
I implore you, even beg, please to me do not relay
You seek to hold against me what God has already forgiven
You seek to expose what from His own memory God has hidden
I walk in liberty when you think that everything is forbidden
I won't be held hostage by the bondage which has captured you
Not taking God's grace for granted
I accept what God is supposed to do
He's in the business of restoration and saving the wayward soul

Convicting through the power of the Holy Spirit
That's His to do not your role
Making the fragmented whole when life has taken its toll
His grace and mercy I extol
You worry about sin's gate and wondering if hell will be my goal
When living a life in Christ is a better pursuit than to manipulate and control
God is more than wise enough to know if your heart is true
You look at the outward and God sees the intents
Much deeper through
You worry about being condemned by God
Christ's righteousness has been imputed to me and also includes you
Yet you still can't see past what you are determined to not understand
Putting demands on my walk with blood stains on your hands
Standing on a foundation broken, shifting, unstable sand
For some reason I'm included in your assessments about what holy should be

When like the woman caught in the act of sin
He made her whole like little old me
The outside is still catching up and God who's my defense
Is patient as He waits an eternity for me
His love will not relent
Knowing I would need His grace before I was even a
glimmer of seed in history
It's a story that you won't believe
A developing testimony
You?
Like the Pharisees and Sadducees balloons blowing hot air
Saying Lord, Lord with the lips but their hearts are far with
empty demonstrative prayers
I want to surrender
Lay everything bare
I want to walk in peace and joy, experience the rare
You have the knowledge but for the Spirit you refuse to
care
You only see the common, familiar
You shout out to be heard in your judgments but
sometimes God speaks by a whisper

Anything different you refuse and refute
You are made blind by expectations adopted which pollute
It dilutes and like rotten fruit, produces no good seed
It clouds your understanding because through man's eyes you referee
Deeming yourself an authority when your jurisdiction only applies to the image of your own reflection
I am the recipient of Christ's affection and I work to fight through the weight of your inspection
I guarantee that should keep you busy enough
Worrying about your own glory to glory
When you are still on page number one God is completing chapters in my story
Keep looking out for your own change
Support me in mine but my life, don't seek to rearrange
Don't force what can only in time unwind
Try to pry apart only what God can unbind
Create me in your image when by Christ I'm being refined
We are all made in His image
By His word alone I am defined

"But godliness with contentment is great gain. For we brought nothing into the world, and we can take nothing out of it. But if we have food and clothing, we will be content with that."

1 Timothy 6:6-8

**Glory 2**

**Singleness**

**vs.**

**Contentment**

## Covenant Love

I want the love of a man who sees me

Feels me

Will not live without me

As he is submitted to Christ

He has made me his priority

He's found me in the serenity of contentment in the Lord

Adored lovingly like Christ does His church

His affection on me he has poured

Ecstatic at the opportunity to make me his very own

Building a home on foundation firm

Never alone

Our bond is reaffirmed in the covenant vows we make

The solid rock of Christ

Terms abiding

This bond we will not break

Everlasting

Commitment unbroken

Not choked by indecision, fear, selfishness unspoken

Selflessness prevails as we hail the God who brought us

together

Facing clear or stormy weather

We have become one and cleave

Each believing God for a love binding

Not reminding or looking for faults

With each other finding favor

Savoring the sweet taste of love

As our spirits connect above soul & flesh

Together in Christ we rest

While tested our connection cannot be severed

We have a connection that is covered, treasured

It can't be measured

More than fond or a passing fancy

Commitment everlasting

## Fairy Tales

3 days

Prince meets princess

Fall in love

Wedding is set

Expectations perfectly met

Release white doves

Happy ever after share love...

Too bad God's promises aren't always fulfilled that way

What do you say is the norm?

To learn to trust the Lord in calm or storm

To seek Him first and rehearse what you expect to become

As you let God "Do what He do"

Waiting

And waiting

And waiting

For your turn at "I do" you wait to be wooed

He wants to pronounce us not just as man and bride

But in Christ to abide

Fairy tales can't compare to God's promises

His infallible yea & amen Word

He is preferred as this desire is deferred

Have you heard His call?

Received His invitation to prepare for the banquet

Learn to feast & be satisfied at His table

And what the flesh desires most

Will become least in His will

And before you know it

Basking in the glow of contentment

And replete in His unrelenting love

The desires of your heart are pulled from eternity to you

Just love the Lord

And let Him "Do what He do"

## Now Whole

Picking up the broken and shattered pieces of me
Widely scattered in bedrooms where I had no home
Heart roaming for love in the wrong places
Chasing when I should have been waiting
Sexing' when I should have been seeking Christ
Deceived by a legitimate need
I believed a man could fill the void
Found my emotions toyed
Spirit destroyed
Annoyed at how I was being treated
Feeling defeated
Yearning for completion
All sorrow needing deletion
Yet not putting my trust in Him who died for me
Shed blood to be
Remission of all sin for me
Spotless lamb bleating to the father to free me
I knew what I was doing
And as guilt ate away while I played at wife
The abundant life God desired for me eluded me
Polluted by a need for a man far greater than my need

for God

I continued to stumble

Made humble by my circumstances

Heart still open, I craved God's love

Needed His acceptance

Redemptive power to restore

More and more I hungered for His righteousness

Longed for His peace

Release from my pain as the pieces of my wounded vessel

Christ gathered at the cross

No longer lost

I am now found

Not bound by the shackles

Of settling for less

No more mess

Only what God shall seek to bless me with is acceptable

Through Christ I have overcome

Am victorious

How glorious I have become since surrendering myself to

the son

Surrendering

Surrendering

No longer rendering myself capable of the work needing to

be done

But letting the ONE

Our tri-un God work through me

Molded in the Potter's hands

Now God's woman

His blood-bought priceless bride

No need to hide

Bowed low in submission, no pride

And I wait...

I wait...

Acknowledging that my desire for a mate still exists

I persist in seeking 1st His kingdom

Insist on letting Christ be the intimate lover of my soul

No longer allowing my temple to be overrun by vandals

But tenderly loved by the man in robes and sandals

God in flesh who died for me

Making whole my broken and shattered pieces

### This Ain't No Dating Thing!

Feelings-Commitment-Ratification

Body-Soul-Spirit connection

Eyes see

Attraction

Courtship

Love grows

Seal the deal

Covenant

Not just cohabitating

But collaborating under Christ centered covenant

Developed out of committed courtship and connected

Spirit

Sharing common goals companions create cohesive connections while walking in collective cooperation only in Christ.

This ain't no dating thing!

Can you dig it?

## What's taking God so long?

Where is my happy ever after?
I thought it was complete in the finished works of Christ on the cross
Yet my emotions only acknowledge my loneliness and feelings of loss
Yes, the Word says I will never be lost or forsaken but these years and years of singleness and unfulfilling relationships have left me shaken
Left and right congratulations & salutations ring in my ear as bling arises on the left index fingers of ladies far and near
Yet...will it ever be my turn I fear?
I am Christ's bride right?
Shouldn't that be enough?
With my heart felt praise and hands raised in worship
I move on tough & trusting in the promise I feel...
Will it ever be real?
Like my expectations, not lofty & vain
Full of hope in white steeds & iron clad knights performing damsel rescuing great deeds
Just a man in love with the Lord, the tangible manifesting

of all God's love stored in flesh for me
See, I have a desire higher than sexual gratification and loving communication
A grander revelation to give God glory in my situation but for now I want to be content
Yet all I can think of is night after night spent alone
No velvet, loving voice to keep me company on the phone
No one dropping me off home after a night of jazz, dancing & moonlit walks on cobblestone
Talking of things spiritual and then some
Mmmmm…
And a daughter's questions and innocent inquiries
Bringing light to conversations only shared in my diaries
"Mommy, what's taking God so long?"

## Contentment

They say still waters run deep

Yet sleep eludes me

The waves of my mind crash

I know my heart has depth

Yet as I wept last night,

Woke up this morning,

with the dew of my tears fresh on my pillow,

I prayed that this day would be abundant in peace and joy

It is clear that I am blessed but in this test I hurt...

I concede that as this God given need goes unmet

I grow weak

Wishing to mount on eagle's wings

I seek for the Lord to speak and I wait

Anticipate the promise being fulfilled

I walk in God's will with perseverance

I pursue Christ in lieu of any doubts

I fight and shout to trust this place I'm in

He's paid the price for the contentment I want to begin

### Christ Saves!

Captain save a sister

Will you come and save my soul

I'm feeling lonely, broken

Can you come and fill this hole?

Wait!

My opinion is beginning to fluctuate

I can't write anymore

Despair no longer do I feel

Something different is knocking at the door

It is quick and real that contentment has been brought

Being sought for so long that it's always in my thoughts

No sad songs

Joy unspeakable is my new tune

No more howling at the moon in misery

Licking peanut butter off a spoon watching murder mysteries

Rejoicing in bliss unspeakable at my peace

Released

I am free

Still able to acknowledge that with a Godly man I'd like to be

Satisfied right now with Christ because He's my strength

My life

I don't need a captain to save me because my Jesus

already has

Blood, shed, risen, redeemed

God's plan in history brought to pass

That request for a captain to save me can't last

Because through Christ, God's only Son, It's done!

I am so blessed

But I'm still alone so back to that request…

## My Promise Land

My Egypt

A land filled with broken promises

Unfulfilled dreams

Unsurpassed expectations

Land of despair, worry and too many cares

and the red sea in front of me...

Moving forward means letting go

Trusting God

Knowing that He will part the waters of my red sea

Doubts, fears and inabilities

The weight of being alone at times crushing me

Overwhelming me

Consumed at the possibility of waters separated

High on either side of me

Crashing down upon me and still He wants my trust

I must move forward

Unlike the children of Israel

Egypt does not look good enough to return to

Yet one of its princes beckons with the promise of

potential

I reckon with my own reason

Wanting to accept this season

Accept the growth necessary past this great divide of fear

and pride

My red sea and on the other side wilderness

Desolate, dry and barren

Place of availability

Creativity

Pain and solitude

Revealed duplicity

Double mindedness, His kindness

Abundant manna and quail

Burning bushes when faith prevails

Overwhelming presence of God in the midst of storm

A calm, peace, bondage released

Wilderness is death and life

Abundance and strife—obedience

My wilderness

And on the other side

My promised land

Already prepared, blessings shared

Giants waiting to be slain

Fertile grounds already lain

Milk and honey flowing free

His true prince waiting for me

No return to Egypt's slavery and the unknown of the red

sea...?

Surrendered

Submitted

Only God's promised land for me

## Done

Letting him go without a kind word or closure

No glance

Or 2nd chance at speaking

Hope slowly leaking

Dying away

Approval removed

Feelings subdued

Loving feelings accrued

Now I rue them and

I

**Am**

**Done!**

Welcoming Christ in with all surrender and joy

No chance or lack of happenstance to seek Him

Bright, no longer faint

Live renewed without restraint

Peace restored

My only Lord

He is my source

I work to be satisfied with Him as my perfect choice

## Resignation

Looking at your face

Praying it will change & that resignation of a relationship

over will take its place

Hoping the lines of hope and care

I once saw in your eyes

Will fade into the ugliness of unacceptability and pain

Yet your glow remains

Is God allowing me to see His good in you?

When all your actions do is cut, destroy and unglue

Was I a mere toy for your lustful desire that I could not

satisfy in my path of purity and purpose?

Was I a passing distraction?

No lasting attraction

Did you see the heart of me?

Or only desire to see how far you could get with me

My only plea was to be loved and accepted

Yet here I find myself again rejected

I say to myself this cannot be

As I prayed to be released from the real you I failed to see

**Memories**

Help me to keep my mind stayed on you Lord
When memories of moments now gone weigh me down
When the frown that seeks to surface
Longing devours purpose
Remind me of your grace and mercy
When I still feel the length of his hand in mine
Time stands still at how real the thought is
Help my strength to be renewed
Subdue my pain
When the sweetness of his kiss, I miss
Shower me with your loving kindness
In my mind I see his eyes
& as I hold back the instinct to cry
It is Your face oh God that brings me joy unspeakable
Peace unreachable through mortal means
It seems so simple
Yet my remembrance of him is fond
Complicates the process of waiting
Those thoughts keep baiting me
And Lord, please don't question my love of you
I'm just being true to what I feel

I see his hand reaching for mine...but that's not real

The dream quickly fades into feelings of

loneliness & misunderstanding

Why couldn't I be the one?

Where is the son in Christ you've destined for me?

Is my desire just a fantasy fueled by my envious eyes and

empty arms?

Grasping at the air

Wishing a Godly man was there...

## Not Giving Up!

Is there no deliverance for a heart weary & worn?

Tired of struggle

Weak and torn

Wanting only to love and be loved in return

What lesson is there to be learned in solitude & pain?

Together we must shoulder the blame

Harness the desire to call names

Heal the hurts and mend our wounds

It's never too soon but can always be too late

Should you procrastinate in saving lost love?

Is it worth the cost?

Sacrifice of pride

To strengthen a bond worn thin to breaking

What are you waiting for?

Should I just give up?

Concede the victory to a selfish heart?

Resign myself to a life alone, abject in misery?

Heavens no!

Not me!

If I allowed that what would my life in Christ be?

Not a sham! Not a mockery!

While I wait trying to push aside what frustrates

A mind gone loopy with longing for affection

Takes off the straight jacket and moves in a different direction

A sweet contentment as I wait on the faithful man with a selfless heart He has for me

Never giving up!

No chance of giving in!

And even when discouraged,

God's spirit, authentic & genuine draws me in...

**Boundaries**

Going farther than I know I should

Dancing on the precipice of sound mind & curiosity

Emotions piqued and flaring

Yet my spirit glaring with growth at the possibility of stumbling

Overlooking the reality briefly

Rational thoughts intercede

Grateful for the love and peace God has given yet...

Ever hopeful that you might be the one

As I am tossed about in the sea of letting all convictions go

Trying to win your love with my affection

Past recollections of a terrible pattern pound my mind

Don't do it!

Don't go down this road again!

Be a friend not a passing distraction

Don't these boundaries cross again

Break the cycle of seeking and chasing

Christ ever present and erasing my guilt stained past

Reminding me always that my body is His temple

Not to be defiled but revered

Not abused but adored

His boundaries are for my protection

This recollection keeps me from stumbling

It's humbling that He remembers my name

Covers and guards me even after my sins

Takes away my shame

I am blameless before Him

Each time I seek to step outside of the protection He provides I remember the importance of

Boundaries

## Something New

Something new and special is in store for me
Extraordinary and exquisite
Yet now it can't be seen
But I can feel the promise in my heart
Blossoming red as Christ's blood
My Rose of Sharon
As beautiful as the love expressed in His sacrifice
I don't have him yet and neither am I his...
Yet the fulfillment of childhood fantasy and adolescent dreams
carried into womanhood remains steadfast
As I have sought first His Kingdom
this desire continues to last
Two shall become one flesh and
so forsaking all he will cleave to me
Although at present I know not who he will be
Most days' content to wait
Not preoccupied with setting wedding dates
Making plans when the whim or fancy comes
Taking notes of the day that covenant comes in
I will no longer in singleness be free

The kind of wife I desire to be

Is it ever too soon to prepare for that which God has spoken you will become?

Someday God's beloved daughter will be united with God's beloved son

And like Adam's rib removed to create Eve

I want to believe experiences lay in wait for me

I will be what he lost and now with God has found

Available to be received

"So I say, live by the Spirit, and you will not gratify the desires of the sinful nature. For the sinful nature desires what is contrary to the Spirit, and the Spirit what is contrary to the sinful nature. They are in conflict with each other, so that you do not do what you want. But if you are led by the Spirit, you are not under law."

Galatians 5:16-18

**Glory 3**

**Lust of the Flesh**

**vs.**

**Surrendering to the Spirit**

## My Hope

My hope is in my surrender
Promise fulfilled as I die in body
Not grieving
Relieved as old man passed away
Gives birth in a new day
Rejoicing in the risen me
Molded into Christ's image
From Glory to Glory
There's life so rich, abundant
I forsook my own
Let Christ live in me
Making my heart His home
Seeking His kingdom foremost, first
Let the fruits of His Spirit burst forth
Let Him work not around but through
Surrender is my key to life complete
Not always neat, but to Him always true
Eternally in order does God work
Putting all the shattered pieces of me together
Binding together what was asunder
I am like clay in His hands as I surrender my hope...

## Depth

Walk in the Spirit

& deny the flesh its evil ways

Submit to authority

& follow what Christ' Spirit says

Under the influence of our desires

Giving in to every beck and call

If you keep seeking to fulfill the flesh,

you're asking for a fall

Don't just visit the Spirit

Live and learn to walk in obedience to Him

Let Him help control your will and talk

Surrender to Him every sin

Condemn every unjust thought

& lean your understanding near

Not to what your body wants to do

but all from Christ you hear

Consumed with searching out the light

Function in death to fleshly whims

And live in abundance with the Lord

Please set your eyes on Him

Keep your mind focused on His words

Get drunk with the Holy Spirit's wine that you have sought

You cannot please your Holy God

If you cannot take captive every single thought

How do you hear the Spirit?

With every seed He planted in you

Your spirit merged with Holy God's

And linked with His thoughts and ways so true

Agreement with the very heart of God

Speaking to you in depths of being real

You know, you know deep down

So strongly rooted, assured you'll grow & heal

**Surrender, not excusing sin...**

Sin creeping
Peep, peep peeping through the door
Having the audacity to be spic n' span clean
Decked out to be seen at church
While the filth of the night before
still lingers under the scent of your cologne
*When will you let Jesus in?*
Taking grace for granted ain't nothin' to you
Spitting in the sacrificial lamb's face is a full time job to do
Saying amen as your eyes scan the room for your next conquest
Tempting those who are truly seeking Christ to fail their tests
*Obedience is better than sacrifice*
While God is desiring intimacy with you
You're being intimate with every six foot, sexy set of six packs that shows you some attention
*Guard your heart & honor your temple which is the Lord's*
Does any of this apply to you?
We all have struggles & temptations, yes

Instead of looking for the nearest way of escape,
You make a home
Basking in the luxury of sin and you don't stay alone
You invite others to wallow in the mud & goo
Staying true to the sin man instead of the Spirit of God in you

*Have you ever invited someone to Jesus?*
Not the club
While in church making a mockery of our blood stained sacrifice
You give place to every vice
And instead of burden sharing
Bearing your sins to the cross
You hide behind tight smiles
All the while watching the clock
Waiting for service to be out
To make that rendezvous your smile is really about
Insincere hugs & meaningless "I'm blessed" are given
as you shrug away the weight of your activity
*What happened to accountability?*

*Do you know that His burden is easy & His yoke is light?*
Don't cry to a friend after the deed is done
Seek flight to avoid giving into the temptation
Sexual sin hails
Bitterness prevails
Jealousy & envy leave behind messy trials
In Adam we all died and yes we're all born in sin
Yet don't excuse it
Allow the life changing power of the Holy Spirit
to spread outward from within
Share Christ's love & gospel truth
No more homosexuality
Double minded duality, tossed about like the waves
Fight the things your flesh craves
Don't give place to neutrality
It's not my business, oh yes it is!
Encourage those around you to follow Christ
Bring a soul to everlasting life
But never at the expense of what His Word says to do
That midnight phone call leading to a creep
That late night visit to the prepaid website before you go

to sleep

That credit card increased limit induced shopping spree

*Please don't take for granted your liberty!*

I know that I sound harsh

Maybe I need to lighten up

But my elephants pink & large as life with me daily use to sup

Yet now I'm being set free and in humility each day

I surrender every bit and all & I pray

Not perfect but I see that sin

Even when secret separates you from God's love

Ask for forgiveness, bring it out in the open

Seek the help you need from Christ's body and above

Don't let a herd of pink elephants keep you from the abundant life for which Christ died

Let His grace be sufficient and let your witness be I tried

And tried

And tried

And tried

Then I surrendered and let the Holy Spirit be my guide

### I Ain't Lookin' Back

I don't want to turn into a pillar of salt
I ain't lookin' back
God didn't come in flesh, suffer and die
So I could stay off track
No sir
My life will be a testimony
To His faithfulness and grace
His mercy has erased every guilty stain
His Holy Spirit comforts every area of pain
His Word is nourishment to my soul
And where I am empty,
He makes me whole
I don't have a choice but to make Him my source
Divorce myself from everything that is contrary to His plan
Following God's prompting
Letting His Spirit lead
Obeying every command
Needing His guidance in every thought, word and deed
I am not looking back at mistakes made
That debt has already been paid
Blood bought

Salvation sought and received

I believe in His restoring power

Each hour of my life is filled with thoughts of His

faithfulness

My desire is to grow closer

No misery

No strife

Only life with my savior

I ain't lookin' back

## Am I Sure...

For once my spirit is fully at peace with whom I've given
my heart
And yet turmoil & confusion surround me
Astound me
Am I sure?
A roadblock to a vision I desire fulfilled
Frustrated at the lingering hope when I know right now
that the season for harvest is far off
I try to meditate on God's promises
Surrender to His spirit
Elevate my mind with His Word and seek His guidance
I want to know His voice clearly when I hear it
Not hiding my face from Him
Yet the face of whom I love hides from me
His visage steals my peace
Makes it difficult for me to believe
God, are you showing me His character?
True nature revealed
Unsealing my eyes so my heart can be healed?
Restoring sight to my blinded soul, mind, will & emotions
Wrapped around a man when they should be reaching for

you

You alone God deserve all of my devotion

Why am I allowing my flesh to create such a commotion?

Forgive me for idolizing that which cannot save

Giving in to my flesh and the companionship I crave

Seeking that which cannot deliver

Draw me near to You

Wash me in the flow of your cleansing river

Keep me from that which fails to sustain me when my

desire to be connected only pains me

Let my joy be complete in Christ

Take over my life as I learn to walk in the spirit and ignore

the deceptive desires of this flesh

## Is That All You Want?

I'm sitting on the sofa
Content and agreeable
All I want to do is converse with you
Maybe watch a movie or two
And then it happens...again...Snap!
Your hand which was just moments ago in your very own
lap
Is inching its way around my neck
Softly caressing my back
I contemplate what's going down
My heart weeps at what I know will come
Damn! Not another one
You're tipping up my chin with your forefinger and the
gentle softness of your thumb
I've made up my mind time and time again
You won't be another one
But boundaries go out the window the minute your touch
hits my skin
I haven't had a relationship in so long
This is not a mess I want to be in

Yet at your mere caress my nerve fibers sing the sweetest song

Every synapsis firing powerful and strong

I connect with you on a level deeper than my flesh

Is it the same for you?

Or am I just another potential conquest?

There is a lesson I have learned that I must remember

Desire burns like a fire, scolding embers

It can rage out of control like it's been starved since last November

I wish you just wanted to talk

Discover the recesses of my mind

Can we just have a conversation?

See what compelling things we can find?

My wit and charm were so attractive to you before

Why has that changed since I've walked through your door?

Is it just my physique that makes you feel complete?

Encouraged you to extend me the invitation to join you on your love seat

I'm suffering from emotional dehydration

Yet filled with the sweetest elation

Admiration for who I think you are...

What a sensation

I don't move

Although I know it would behoove me

Be in my best interest to get far from you

I guarantee

What are you doing girl?

Why are you still here?

Why must you continue to trust your flesh?

What is it that you fear?

Then a thought crosses my mind

It persists in lingering

Maybe I'm not the issue

I put up my emotional tissue

My own reasoning I'm fingering

Manipulating

Trying to figure out

Start to think about the root issues

What this is really all about

What harm is there in believing that a guy really just wants to chat?

Is it naivety to see the innocence in others?

Where is the sin in that?

I want to live holy...

Men nowadays

That will run them off in no time flat

See...

I try and try, again and again to believe that intentions have honor

In the temptation of sex, is our courtship a goner?

Does our friendship have to be thrown out when longing pops up?

From the cup of physical pleasure do we have to sup?

Meek and gentlemanly before

You're now passionately pursuing more

Your hand is slowly caressing my face

Soon your lips take hands place

Soft kisses to my cheek

This is beginning to feel bleak

I really want to get up and leave

Can I truly believe you wanted to get to know me?
When as you are pulling me closer only your passion I see
Again, is it me or the new reality?
Do what feels good
What are you waiting for?
That Bible stuff is outdated
Don't be a bore
All that purity and celibacy stuff is just spiritual lore
Your kisses have moved from my cheeks to my lips
They are soft, firm yet gentle
Your tongue, I feel the tip
From my mouth you urgently, fiercely sip
It feels good but that is where I want to stop
I'm content to kiss and let any other notions drop
Your hands keep migrating
You are persistent
Relentless in making me breathless
I feel defenseless at the complete lack of control in my senses
Yet in my mind my spirit and soul are in complete consensus

Run, escape, flee...
You've given it a little more time and no change this chance
You are determined to make your advance
The quiet voice in me is now screaming,
Did you hear me girl?!? Are you listening to me?
I said leave!!!
It's been fun bruh but the vow I made...
My commitment to remain pure
All the nights I have prayed
Is more important than this temporary surge of allure
I don't want to be premature
Engage in behavior that only marriage is designed for
Been there
Done that
I want to be in a relationship committed and secure
I am not helpless and abandoned to this desire
I've been given a way to escape temptations fire
I decide to use my free will and take it
No making decisions that break my spirit
I disentangle myself from your welcomed embrace

Gauge the distance from me to the door so I can get out of your place
I adjust my dress and stand
Lord I need to get away from this man
My conviction is now making its demands
Politely excuse myself from our compromising position
My will is surrendering to God's way of its own volition
For holiness I must stand
I look you in the eyes and with fear, sorrow, & determination say that I can't
Whether you understand or not will speak to me if you're a real man
A million thoughts run through my mind
It's hard to pull away from your touch
For you, my presence is an enticement, too much
I want to continue to sit and talk but I know that I cannot
I give a hug and one last kiss
My stomach is in knots
My heart it aches, it's sad
The question remains as I lock your gaze
Is sex all you want and will I hear from you again?

But the Lord said to Samuel, "Do not look on his appearance or on the height of his stature, because I have rejected him. For the Lord sees not as man sees: man looks on the outward appearance, but the Lord looks on the heart."

1 Samuel 16:7

**Glory 4**

**Bondage of Religion**

**vs.**

**Liberty of Relationship**

## Worship Not Religion

No religion welcome here
Relationship is what He truly desires
To see souls on fire for Him
Not diminished in worship
Lights hid under bushels of pomp and circumstance
So caught up in ceremony and tradition
For the Lord you can't dance
Stiff and at attention you clap your hands politely
Worship and praise to God is not something to take lightly
Forget about who's around you
Wanting to appear proper and prim
Do you have even an ounce of His Awesome Spirit within?
I can't imagine not worshipping my great redeemer
Savior and healer with full, inexhaustible energy
Because I am a believer and He has set me free
The song says you don't know my story yet I can clearly see yours
It's apparent at your lack of reverence for worshipping the Lord

I can't imagine a full awareness of the greatness of our God
All you can manage during songs of praise is a half-hearted smile and nod
When you should be hollering out His glory all you can give him is an applaud?
Ram rod straight and praise sedate
To celebrate Him you have to be prod
I close my eyes to bask in the presence of the Lord
So as to not be discouraged by the expression on your face, weary and bored
Where is your courage for worshipping the Lord?
Does legalism and regulations control your every thought?
Do you look around to see if someone has the dress you bought?
You can sit on the pew for hours but without true worship it's for not
The warmth of your bottom on the seat does not celebrate the Lord
Your religion doesn't honor God
Do you know He should be adored?

## Distortion

Teacher,
You preaching prosperity theology but the only one
prospering is you
Folks in your congregation are broke
So weary and in need of clothes, shoes and food
You're driving the latest model Benz
Armani suits are tailored to fit your form
You distort the meaning of the scriptures
For yourself creating a violent storm
You promise blessing and favor in lives
If members give all they have to you
Yet the seed they plant is in grounds of lies
As you mutilate God's Word of truth
How can you ignore the scriptures principals of
contentment, love and regardless of the amount, cheerful
giving?
Instead you focus on material things
like flat screens, houses, cars and fancy living
Men & women of eager means who want to show great
faith
Use food money or take a portion of rent

to pay for God's favor and grace

Hocking bottles of blessed oil, anointed crosses,

water from the Jordan and prayer cloths

Deceiving people desperate for a touch from the Lord with

gimmicks

when in the blood they need to be washed

You better take serious the gospel you preach

The shaky ground on which you stand

For all those who listen to your distorted message

Their blood is on your hands

Don't take lightly the authority you have

to influence for the Kingdom and Christ

There are people out there who need a savior

In your possession is the rest of their lives

## Freedom in Christ

Let me get straight to it!
The weight of others critical group imposed standards has become too heavy to bear.
Dare I not speak my mind and be God's masterpiece creatively expressive?
Fear of judgment based on the outer not the inner tried to cripple me
I have been set free and will not be bound by chains found and embraced in others so called walks.
You be fully convinced in what you believe and do but to put it on another is to crush their liberty and confuse Christ's truth.
Rapper-spit your verses!
Dancer-leap your jete!
Poetess-write with abandon!
Pianist-with passion play!
God has gifted us all to walk in individuality in His plan.
Don't be distracted or hindered to change your course due to the fallible opinion of man.
Be all that God has created you to be
There is an inability in many to misunderstand

You command attention in all you do

Of course for His glory

You are exceptionally made by Christ's hand.

Workmanship wonderful & writer of poetry eloquent

Masterpiece priceless

His beloved delicate & made with so intricate….

You operate in your liberty in Christ!

## You've Been a Friend

Relationship with you God is the pinnacle of friendships
Father, blessed covering
Son, redemptive Savior
Holy Spirit, comforting presence
Reminiscing of days when You were not enough
Yet grateful that fellowship with You has always been available
There is nothing that I could have done to win Your love and affection
No sacrifice made
No plans laid
No debt paid that could make me more acceptable to You
Christ has already done what I could never do
Still I desire to dedicate all I am to worship and serve
Make me righteous, holy
Already justified
Being sanctified
Looking to be glorified
When wearing the right thing or observing the right tradition didn't work
Your blood accomplished much, enough

More than I could deserve

Nothing is greater than a friend laying his life down for another

&

You have done more

Been a provider, confidant, brother

Bearing my burdens and sharing my load-heavy

Steady and consistent in my life

What a friend I have in You, Jesus Christ...

Accepting me

Loving even when I can't see

Abiding when I am not worthy

Faithful even as I struggle to consistent be

Gifting me with incredible gifts of freedom, liberty

Not for free

You paid the penalty

Yet with no additional expectation from me

So I can with a heart light and with no burden or obligation

Surrender my heart and life to You

Making myself available to consecration

## Sometimes I Wonder

Sometimes I wonder what it would be like to be free
To walk in complete openness and true liberty
To share what I've been given with charity and love
To express my hearts worship received on Earth and above
To not be fearful of envy or jealous prejudice or pride
To believe that the person telling me no is authentic and not their true intentions trying to hide
Leadership who tries to convince me to wait on God but in your own words do you abide?
I often find in the church that we manipulate and control
Getting their own needs and agenda's met is often the only goal
Guised under the hand of God and we are told to trust Him to work it out
When leadership are the ones with the ability to move as His hands
What is that all about?
So you make others feel bad for speaking
For being honest and doing what the word says
Taking your issues to your brother but you let it go to your head

Every question isn't an affront to your sovereignty
Every concern isn't an attack against you
Every conversation isn't an opportunity for you to validate your authority
That's not always what you have to do
I wonder if in the church of Christ, we really took the time
To highly esteem the other just the change that we would find
People wouldn't leave their churches except for opportunities to develop and to grow
Anger and strife wouldn't seethe under the surface as folks talk behind your back
If you never change things how will you know?
You try to convince that your intentions are pure but the discerning heart that I own
Knows deep down inside that those are all lies
Do you realize the hurt that you've sown?
Are you even aware yourself of the deception that you communicate?
Or have you blown smoke up others rears for so long that you believe all the stuff you ruminate?

I wonder if you've really contemplated the predicament
that you have put so many in?
Can I ask that and just be blunt?
Tell the truth
So many abandoning their true hearts desires while you
set your own talents up front
If not for the desire to honor God and worship Him in spirit
and truth
If I did not seek to bless the Lord in worship, I promise I
would not fool around with you
My heart is so hurt and wounded
Because you seem to be blocking my purpose
worthless

"My brethren, count it all joy when you fall into various trials, knowing that the testing of your faith produces patience. But let patience have its perfect work, that you may be perfect and complete, lacking nothing."

James 1:2-4

**Glory 5**

**Worry & Uncertainty**

**vs.**

**Patience & Purpose**

## The Deposit

There are no words to express purpose deposited and a
longing to see destiny released
A peace overwhelms because with God at the helm I know
I will become all He desires
My heart on fire for Him
No longer giving place to every whim I wait
Placated by the comfort of His Holy Spirit, warm embrace
Knowing that every cry He hears it!
Yes, He hears it!
And uncertainty?
There's no need to fear it
Although it frequently makes its presence known
I can't let it make a home in my heart
I start daily praising and practicing
Reminded by the Holy Spirit of all I have to be thankful for
Even though the doubts sometimes come more & more
God pours greater depths of Himself into me
Preparing me for His plans
Those things He's gifted me to do that bring Him glory
I stand using my story as a testimony of His grace & mercy
As I wait for His purpose deposited in me to be revealed

**I AM**

I am exceptional

Anointed

By God appointed

Set apart

Made fearfully—in reverence, awe

Wonderfully—In excellence I am called

New creation

Proverbs 31 made

Reaping in abundance through the sacrifice Christ made

Qualities of spring

Warm as April showers

Yet summer harvest coming overflowing in God's power

Did you hear?

Ephesians, my Father's workmanship

A masterpiece

All former names gone by

Cease

Replaced by

Cut above the rest

Passing every test

Head & not the tail

Through every trial prevails
Bountiful blessing is God's destiny for me
Not in the flesh but that which reveals His glory
Unwavering in my desire to see Him glorified
To Him consecrated
Me sanctified
Frequent moments of weakness
Do I experience day to day?
Yet in it He's stronger for His power to display
I'm saved for works in Christ Jesus
To testify of abundant mercy & grace
And in my face reflected brightly is His love
As I bask in His presence in praise
For He's made me exceptional
Anointed
By Him I'm appointed
I am set apart

## Expectation

Wait

Hmph, wait

I like that word

Defined by Webster's as:

"to stay in place"

"in expectation of"

"a delay"

But what does my God say?

Be still

Don't grow weary in well doing when circumstances bleary overwhelm

Know I am at the helm

I say peace & calm the waves in your storm

When the world's norm is to worry first, fret and trust last

Your best bet is to first trust Me and believe

That I reward those who in diligence seek me

Wait

See the salvation of the righteous

Stand still

Know that I am God

No façade or charade can mask me

Don't try to rush ahead of my plans

It only leads to misery

More unwanted circumstance

Just be...

Allow me, the sovereign God

To do what I do

In the process of time I will remember you

Wait

**Wait on the Lord!**

What else can I do but wait on you?
Soaring eagle high
Mounted on wings
Not growing weary as in you I fly
Treading life peacefully as storms persist
Able to overcome with Christ's power to enlist
His Word never changing
Although I am born in flesh
Christ has been from beginning
Helps me pass all life's tests
My strength is renewed as in Him do I trust
Operating in His holiness
Not my own selfish lusts
Yet sometimes overcome by the strong emotion I feel
Oh praise God for His comfort that surrounds me
He's real!!!
So I walk and I run though sometimes I do get weary
I feel like I'm fainting then I hear your voice clearly

Wait on the Lord!

## Reign

Focus on the blessing not the deceit of the curse

The enemy would have you dwell in the pain and past

And only think of the worst

The blood-shed pain felt by Christ reversed the

consequences of the cards dealt

Death

Doom & destruction

Roaming lion seeking to devour

Now defeated!!!

Abundant life is ours

Walk in it

Freedom from a past full of mistakes

Abundant life loosed from heartache

Although the consequences of sins past still maintain

In God's grace you reign

In His mercy you can hide

For all you seek to be in Him, rest in Him, abide

Seated on the right hand of the Father

Making intercession for us

We reign in Christ Jesus

In Him put your trust

## Transition

I know that you are not a God of confusion
But right now I'm fighting
The delusion of peace
The allusion of sleep
Leaning not to my understanding but waiting for my ways
to acknowledge you
Still unsure of what to do or where I am going
I'm that great thing waiting to be found
Godly wisdom sound
Who I am desires to reach for your ways
Make the seek a little easier
Smooth and without fault
Yet in my flesh faults is all I seem to have
As I transition from this glory to another what I see
brightly reflected in this mirror of your perfection is lacking
Still I see the silver lining of your Spirit overshadowing
every broken place in me
Making me brand new
Restored and true
No longer wanting to fight against this body of death I rest
in your sweet peace

All you have called me to be and do
Strengthen me to not waiver or faint
As my flesh only seeks to say what I can't
I'm fighting the anxiety when I know that your truth
Speaks peace to my storms and a new calm is produced
Sadly, though it doesn't stay
You remind me consistently day to day
That these transitions are part of the journey
You are developing my character superbly

### Conceding My Will...

Pain

Possibility

Walking in obedience

Although the end I can't see

Rain

Responsibility

Making wise choices

Letting the Lord always lead

Oppose

Agreement

Aligning with God

Sacrificing my will for His

Surrender

Sacrifice

Never defeated

On His promises I do live

Faith

Expectation

Willing to wait

On the perfect will of my Father

Believing

Conceding

All my desires

With my plans I won't bother

## Why Worry?

Why worry when all that is significant has been completed?
It is finished!
Why seek and strive for the temporary when the eternal is within reach?
Touch It!
Seek first His kingdom and all that is worthy of the Will of God is yours…
Not the material but the spiritual
That which makes foundations strong
Patience long and brings joy to song
Does worry add years to your existence or money to your purse?
Does rehearsing the trials of this world
bring any satisfaction to those areas lacking?
Why not just trust the Lord?
With assurance, certainty, confidence hope
With sureness, faith, expectation in Him, cope
Don't dwell on the negative or assume the worst,
It'll make you burst in discouragement
On things noble, honest and in purity dwell

Let hope in Christ grow and doubt dispel
Let the depth of your heart swell...
with thoughts lovely
good in report
heavy in virtue and worthy of praise
Let your days be filled with the love and abundance
that Christ died for and that we all long
As He is knocking at the door
let Him in and don't worry
There is no hurry in forcing the will of Him who loves us
sacrificially
I offer a dare!
On Him cast all your cares

## Whose Confused?

Questions?

Concerns?

Burning thoughts in my mind

Needed lessons to be learned?

Answers I need to find

I am not sure

Things that once seemed so simple

Now doubt cripples

I examine everything I thought I ever knew

What I once thought true

Just stories to keep our hope alive

Or living testimonies to our lives applied

In tears I wonder is God real

Is this just emotion or His presence I feel?

If I express these quandaries that I have

Would the body of Christ laugh?

Dismiss my fears with cliché remarks

Reasons why I would depart

Often I seek to separate

I don't question that God is real

I ask how does He relate?

Are we delusional in what we believe?

Or is He as accessible as we perceive?

Am I confused about who you are God?

No, I don't think so...

In my faith I want to grow

I want these seeds in me to explode

But I sure have some questions and I wanted you to know

"Grace and peace to you from him who is, and who was, and who is to come...
"I am the Alpha and the Omega," says the Lord God, "who is, and who was, and who is to come, the Almighty."

Revelation 1:4-8


**Glory 6**

**Character of Christ**

## Enthroned

God you are enthroned on the praises of Your people
High and lifted up
Running over and above is the cup of Your blessing
While You fill the sanctuary of our hearts the train of Your robe fills the temple
Your monumental nature is fundamental to all we believe
You are Holy, Holy, Holy
Hallowed and divine
All You are redefines who we are
Adopted us into Your bloodline
God over all heaven and Earth
Universe and Stars
Galaxies bow down to the awesomeness of who you are
Our souls the reservoir for your goodness and grace
We embrace the majesty we see in the glory of your face
The ground we stand on is revered because you are here
Your renown and distinction endures through all generations
Your reputation the prominence of your excellence
Your name alone has all precedence
There is no other before You

god, little g

man or beast

all former, forthwith, and future next to You is least

We envision You on Your thrown

We are never alone because You never leave us

Whether we feel it or not Your ways trustworthy and just

Your understanding is so much higher than ours

We were not there when you laid the foundations of the

Earth

Only You knit our bodies together before our birth

Infinite value and worth you've given

Prostrate in humble adoration at Your feet

You defeated death, hell and the grave so we could be

complete

Seeing all omniscience

Omnipotent all power

Seconds building into minutes

Minutes to hours

Weaving throughout history and time

Hours to days

Days to weeks

Valleys and mountain peaks

Your technique in moving through the seasons is explicit,

precise

Working behind the scenes in our life

We worship because there is no one like you Sovereign

God

Guarding over us

You who knew us before the cornerstone was laid

In the surrender of Christ on the cross our debt was paid

We are saved because Holy God in flesh obeyed

We are consecrated for your adoration and praise

You are enthroned in the exultation of your people

## Relentless

Relentless love

Unyielding pursuit

Pure in its devotion

No trial can dilute

Steady in persistence

Never ceasing

Abundant in power

Ever increasing

Relentless love

Christ's love

God in flesh from above

Crucified for our salvation

Love

Incomparable

Unfathomable

Ever available

Inexhaustible

His love for us

So much

No earthly experience can touch

If we would yield

Surrender to His will

Any void He can fill

If we would yet be still

Let His presence be real and relevant

Relentless love

Sweat drops of blood love

Veil of the temple ripped from top to bottom love

Bringing us above every trial & temptation

His love

Crown of thorns on savior born

Bearing bruises and stripes

He didn't gripe

Said they knew not what they did

Received a penalty so severe

God the Father's face turned

From His Son He hid

In sin can't be near

Yet in holding us most dear

Made the message clear

That His love for us first, foremost

Cannot be opposed

Deepest and from the innermost

All heavenly hosts in Him boast

Relentless love

Endless devotion

A sacrifice innocent

Put our salvation in motion

Enduring and faithful

Fulfilling in power

Inexhaustible authority

In His grace showered

Christ's love

God in flesh from above

Crucified for our salvation

Love

### His Face...

The softer side of grace

Can you picture the Savior's face?

No,

Not color, tint of eye or skin

But love expressed outward from within

Hair wavy, smooth or kinked like wool

Don't allow the physical to fool

Blinded by culture

See the spotless lamb

His true purpose, divine

His face glows in the fulfillment of God's plan and it is

finished

Can you see His face?

Disgraced with a crown of thorns

Blood drenched

Forlorn and eyes downcast

Yet glory on the way, the pain would not last

They knew not what they did and from their sin

God hid as veil was rent

His last breath spent

Can you envision our Savior's face?

## Rhema

You're my personal God
Messages just for me
Rhema Word
Heart heard and I receive
Believe and desire to achieve all you have for me
Moving forward in this race of life I press onward
Only going forwards, towards Your goals for me
Not my own
Seeing a glimpse of Your glory in my life
You are faithful, always stable, never changing
The same yesterday, today and forever more
In your love saved me and the grave I no longer fear
Because life abundant I have on earth
Eternity with you is near
Your Word makes my path so clear
All I have to do is be available in seeking you
Your kingdom first
All else in Your will shall be added
Each song never feels just the same
Rhema for Theresa, Rhema for Theresa
My personal God who sends every message with my name

## Great God!

How great God is!
Mighty listener to my troubles
He hears every plea
Strong tower
Open to my cry and able to lift me
Done sifting me like wheat but restore me to
completeness in Him
All He desire to see in me
Rescuing & saving me from the muck & mire
Solid rock foundation
He frees me from sin
Round the clock
Never leaving or forsaking me
Path firm and progress steady
Healer & counselor
God of my today
Shaper of history
Finding comfort in His Word
Keeps me ready and equipped for every good work
I am in awe of Him
Head down humble, I worship in reverence

Of His greatness there is recognition

All deference to God above in quiet submission

I worship as my name He calls…Theresa

Lord, here I am

Send me…to my knees I fall

Open and available because I trust you for the ram in the bush

Every doubt and fear you squash

God, how great you are!

**Chains**

I am desperate to escape the chains of bitterness
These strongholds that bind
Seek to confine me
Imprison me & tightly fetter me
These chains, these strongholds and lofty mindsets
Seek to set themselves up against the Godhead
I demolish those arguments trying to set up monuments in
my mind
Attempting to take those thoughts captive is very hard I
find
Those maladaptive, hyperactive ideas planted by the
deceiver
Those speculations aimed to disarm the believer
Depression, despair and heaviness of heart
Animosity, discord, enmity depart
Jealousy & envy running rampant to destroy me
Blinding me from having faith in the blessings God has for
Me
Me
Me
But it's not about me

He

He

He shed His blood

He showed His love

In that while I was still a sinner He died for me and it was enough

In all my freedom His father gets glory above

I'm rough but He is gentle in His regard towards me

I am obedient in sweeping the debris of this shattered life into the sea of His forgiveness

In every struggle that I surrender to Him I bask in His attentiveness

Every crushing sinful whim and burden that binds me in stagnation

Is released in the arms of His explosive, abiding relations

He

He

He sent His Son whose race finished is won

I have the benefit of walking in the freedom of what He has begun

Indulging in His mercy

Relishing in His grace

Knowing that even in my imperfection through Him I have

a place-A home

I am adopted in Christ

I battle and war against things immoral

Yet in Him there is new life

He

He

He left His Holy Spirit to be a Guide for me

So that blinded occasionally by the vices of the enemy

I don't have to commit spiritual felonies

He brings all things to my remembrance as in His Word I

study

So that every life style choice, depraved and sundry

Are not tempting for me to wallow like pigs all muddy

I can only express my joy that the chains encasing my

heart

Have been disbanded through the blood of Christ

What He's done I can't discard

## He is Christ

No questions, qualifications or hesitations
Deliberations or reservations
No elaboration needed but a declaration
He deserves all adoration
He alone is the Revelation
The embodiment of the Holy and Righteous
Worthy of celebration God
He is the illumination not of our sins but our justification
Salvation-Revelation-Illumination-Transformation
Christ is our Inspiration
The fleshy manifestation
Holy Interpretation
Regeneration of a triune God who needs no preparation
Present in the beginning He is the proliferation of all creation
Emmanuel God with us
Burning bush guidance of a chosen Nation
Greater than the sands of the earth
Yes, multiple generations
No Exaggeration
Sent for the total obliteration of sin and satan's hold

An abomination needing reparation
Our disobedience a damnation
In Adam all died
In consideration of our feeble flesh
Father, Son and Holy Spirit had a collaboration
Decided that our separation was no less an aberration but
a doorway to the evaporation of all our evil ways
Instead of paying us with the reciprocation needed
He forfeits our tribulation through an illustration of His
love
The proliferation of unmerited grace, favor and mercy
No longer strangers we have been grafted in through
immigration
An inauguration took place
The stipulation
Accepting His Son who died on the cross for the
propitiation of your sins
So with exhilaration and all of our corroboration
For eternity drowning in exhalation
He Is Christ!!

Dear God,

I thank you for being my heavenly Father! I thank you for your correction and compassion. I am grateful for your love and the lessons I have learned. Thank you for the things in life that you have allowed that have challenged me in my faith, strengthened it and pulled me ever closer to you even when I had lost all hope.

This book is for your glory and honor. That those who seek first Your kingdom would be encouraged, empowered, edified, and enlightened to seek you at a deeper level. Let us remember that you often use storms to build this character in us. Lord continue to do the work in us that needs to be done. Even in the body of death that I am seeking freedom from, I am still your masterpiece, lovingly sculpted in Your image.

Your daughter,
Theresa

***Scriptures to offer hope and encouragement and build faith!*** *(I encourage reading the scriptures in full context)*

### Colossians 1:13, 14

"For He has rescued us from the dominion of darkness and brought us into the kingdom of the Son He loves, in whom we have redemption, the forgiveness of sins."

### Colossians 2:9

"For in Christ all the fullness of the Deity lives in bodily form, and you have been given fullness in Christ."

### Hebrews 10:17

"Their sins and lawless acts I will remember no more."

### Ephesians 1:4-5,7

"For He chose us in Him before the creation of the world to be holy and blameless in his sight. In love He predestined us to be adopted as His sons through Jesus Christ...In Him [Christ] we have redemption through His blood the forgiveness of sins."

**Ephesians 2:6**

"And God raised us up with Christ and seated us with Him in the heavenly realms in Christ Jesus."

**Ephesians 2:18**

"For through Him [Jesus] we have access to the Father by one Spirit."

**John 14:27**

"Peace I leave with you; My peace I give you. I do not give to you as the world gives. Do not let your hearts be troubled and do not be afraid."

**Philippians 4:7**

"The peace of God, which transcends all understanding, will guard your hearts and your minds in Christ Jesus."

**1 John 4:10**

"In this is love: not that we loved God, but that He loved us and sent His Son to be the propitiation (the atoning sacrifice) for our sins."

**Isaiah 49:15, 16**

"Can a mother forget the baby at her breast and have no compassion on the child she has borne?
Though she may forget, I will not forget you! See I have engraved you on the palms of my hands."

**Matthew 12:50**

"Whoever does the will of my Father in heaven is my brother and sister and mother."

**Romans 3:21, 22**

"But now a righteousness from God...has been made known... This righteousness from God comes through faith in Jesus Christ to all who believe."

**Romans 5:1**

"Since we have been justified through faith, we have peace with God through our Lord Jesus Christ."

**Romans 6:23**

"For the wages of sin is death, but the gift of God is eternal life in Christ Jesus our Lord."

***Romans 8:15-16***

*"You received the Spirit of son ship. And by Him we cry 'Abba, Father.' If we are children, then we are heirs - heirs of God and co-heirs with Christ, if indeed we share in His sufferings in order that we may also share in His glory."*

***Romans 8:38, 39***

*In a time of great struggle and suffering, Paul declared: "I am convinced that neither death nor life,*
*neither angels nor demons, neither the present nor the future, nor any powers, neither height nor depth, nor anything else in all creation, will be able to separate us from the love of God that is in*
*Christ Jesus our Lord."*

Theresa Marie Cain is an early childhood educator in Texas. She is a graduate of the University of Missouri-Columbia. She is also the mother of a beautiful daughter named Iyana Imanii. She serves in the Dance, Choir and Creative Tyme ministries at her church Oak Cliff Bible Fellowship as well as volunteering in other areas as needed. Theresa is very busy enjoying God's gift of life and working to patiently await her Adam.

**Want to contact her?**
ccdelta@yahoo.com
Locate her on Facebook and YouTube under Theresa Marie Cain

www.ingramcontent.com/pod-product-compliance
Lightning Source LLC
Chambersburg PA
CBHW061444040426
42450CB00007B/1199